UNDERSTANDING AMERICAN DEMOCRACY

FREEDOM OF SPEECH AND THE PRESS

by Samantha S. Bell

BrightPoint Press

San Diego, CA

BrightPoint Press

an imprint of ReferencePoint Press, Inc.
Printed in the United States

For more information, contact:
BrightPoint Press
PO Box 27779
San Diego, CA 92198
www.BrightPointPress.com

LIBRARY OF CONGRESS CATALOGING-IN-PUBLICATION DATA

Name: Bell, Samantha S., author.
Title: Freedom of speech and the press / by Samantha S. Bell.
Description: San Diego, CA: ReferencePoint Press, 2024 | Series: Understanding American democracy | Audience: Grades 7-9 | Includes bibliographical references and index.
Identifiers: ISBN: 9781678206949 (hardcover) | ISBN: 9781678206956 (eBook)
The complete Library of Congress record is available at www.loc.gov.

CONTENTS

AT A GLANCE

- Freedom of speech is the right to speak, write, or voice ideas and opinions. This right is essential for a democratic society.
- Freedom of the press is the right to publish information and opinions. This may be through newspapers, magazines, radio, TV, or the internet.
- Freedom of speech and the press is guaranteed by the US Constitution. This document explains how the government works. The first ten amendments to the Constitution are called the Bill of Rights. These protect the rights of people in the United States.
- There are limits to freedom of speech. These limits may be based on when something is said, where it is said, and the way it is said.
- The government cannot restrict someone's speech. But private companies can restrict speech in areas they control.

- Freedom of speech and the press is often challenged during wartime. The safety of the country's people and armed forces become priorities.
- Journalists use freedom of the press to inform people about what the government is doing. This helps hold the government responsible for its actions.
- The Supreme Court has ruled on many cases involving freedom of speech and the press. These cases try to clarify the limits on these freedoms.
- Today, people and the courts are still figuring out these freedoms. Some questions involve speech on college campuses and cameras in courtrooms.

INTRODUCTION

WITHIN THEIR RIGHTS

Jessica stomped into class. "I can't believe it!" she said. She thumped down in her seat.

"What's the matter?" asked Mr. Daniels, her history teacher.

"I've been following my favorite movie star on social media," Jessica began. "Now he's not on there anymore. I read that he was banned for something he said. Whatever happened to freedom of speech?”

“That’s a good point,” Mr. Daniels said. “Class, should social media sites be allowed to ban people?”

Social media companies, such as Twitter and Facebook, can ban people for using speech that goes against their rules.

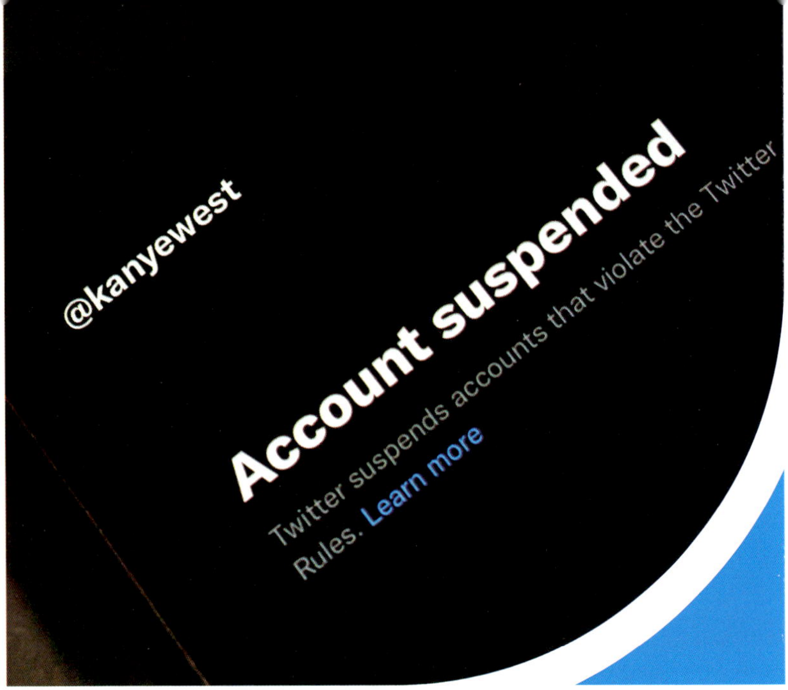

People may be banned from social media sites for using hateful speech or spreading false information.

"No way!" Jessica said.

"But what if the person is lying?" Owen asked.

"Or what if that speech is hateful toward someone?" asked Melissa.

Jessica wasn't sure. She hadn't thought about that before.

“These are good questions,” Mr. Daniels said. “They are some of the questions that the courts must decide. What do you think about someone being banned from a social media site?”

“It’s illegal!” said Jessica.

“Actually, the site can do it,” Mr. Daniels corrected. “The right to freedom of speech applies to the US government. But private companies can ban whomever they choose.”

“Maybe that could be the topic for my report,” said Jessica. “I’ll start by doing some research at the library.”

US citizens have the right to speak and write freely. They can publish their opinions in magazines, newspapers, and other media.

"I like that idea," said Mr. Daniels. Then the bell rang. "OK, class," said Mr. Daniels. "It's time for me to use my freedom of speech. Get ready to take some notes."

EXPRESSING YOURSELF

Jessica knew all Americans had the right to freedom of speech. This is the right to speak freely. Freedom of the press is related to freedom of speech. It means expressing oneself through publications. This includes newspapers and magazines. It also includes websites.

Freedom of speech and the press is important for a **democratic** country. But as Jessica discovered, there are limits to these freedoms. The limits serve to protect these freedoms. They make it possible for everyone to enjoy them.

1

WHAT IS FREEDOM OF SPEECH?

The US Constitution protects freedom of speech and the press. The Constitution was created in 1787. It set up the US government and its powers. It is the highest law of the land.

As of 2023, twenty-seven amendments had been made to the Constitution.

Amendments are changes or additions. The first ten amendments are called the Bill of Rights. These amendments protect people's rights. They keep the government from taking away those rights.

Freedom of speech and the press is included in the First Amendment to the US Constitution.

THE FIRST AMENDMENT

The First Amendment says:

> *Congress shall make no law respecting an establishment of religion, or prohibiting the free exercise thereof; or abridging the freedom of speech, or of the press; or the right of the people peaceably to assemble, and to* ***petition*** *the Government for a redress of grievances.*[1]

This lists several freedoms. People can choose their own religion. They can gather for protests. They can tell the government when something is wrong.

Under the First Amendment, people have the right to participate in peaceful protests.

Freedom of speech and the press is also included in the First Amendment. This means the government cannot punish people for speaking or writing what they think. The United States was built on ideas of freedom and democracy. The First Amendment protects these ideas. But sometimes laws do not match

Journalists have the right to report on government news. This keeps the public informed about the government's actions.

society's values. When this happens, people must be able to speak out.

Freedom of the press helps journalists. It allows them to question government leaders about their actions. Journalists report on events in newspapers or on TV. They can report on leaders who behave badly. This keeps the public informed.

LIMITS ON THE FREEDOMS

The First Amendment allows people to write what they want. But there are some limits to this. False statements can hurt someone's **reputation**. The First Amendment does not protect these statements. False written statements are called libel. False statements that are spoken are slander.

Oher limits to free speech protect privacy. They also protect public safety and national security. The time, place, and manner of speech are limited. For example, a person cannot give a loud speech in the middle of the night. This limits the time. People cannot hold protests that block traffic. This rule limits the place. Protesters cannot harass people or force them to listen by blocking

TELLING TALES

The terms *libel* and *slander* refer to false statements about others. But these terms do not apply if a person says something false about himself. For example, politicians may lie about themselves during campaigns. They may do this to get more votes. Under the First Amendment, they have the freedom to do so.

their way. This involves manner, or the way something is spoken.

These limits keep things running smoothly. They also protect people. For example, people cannot tell military secrets. If enemies knew these secrets, it would put the country in danger. Threats to commit crimes can also be punished. So can fighting words, or insults that may lead to fights. There are limits on what businesses can say too. For example, companies cannot make false statements about their products.

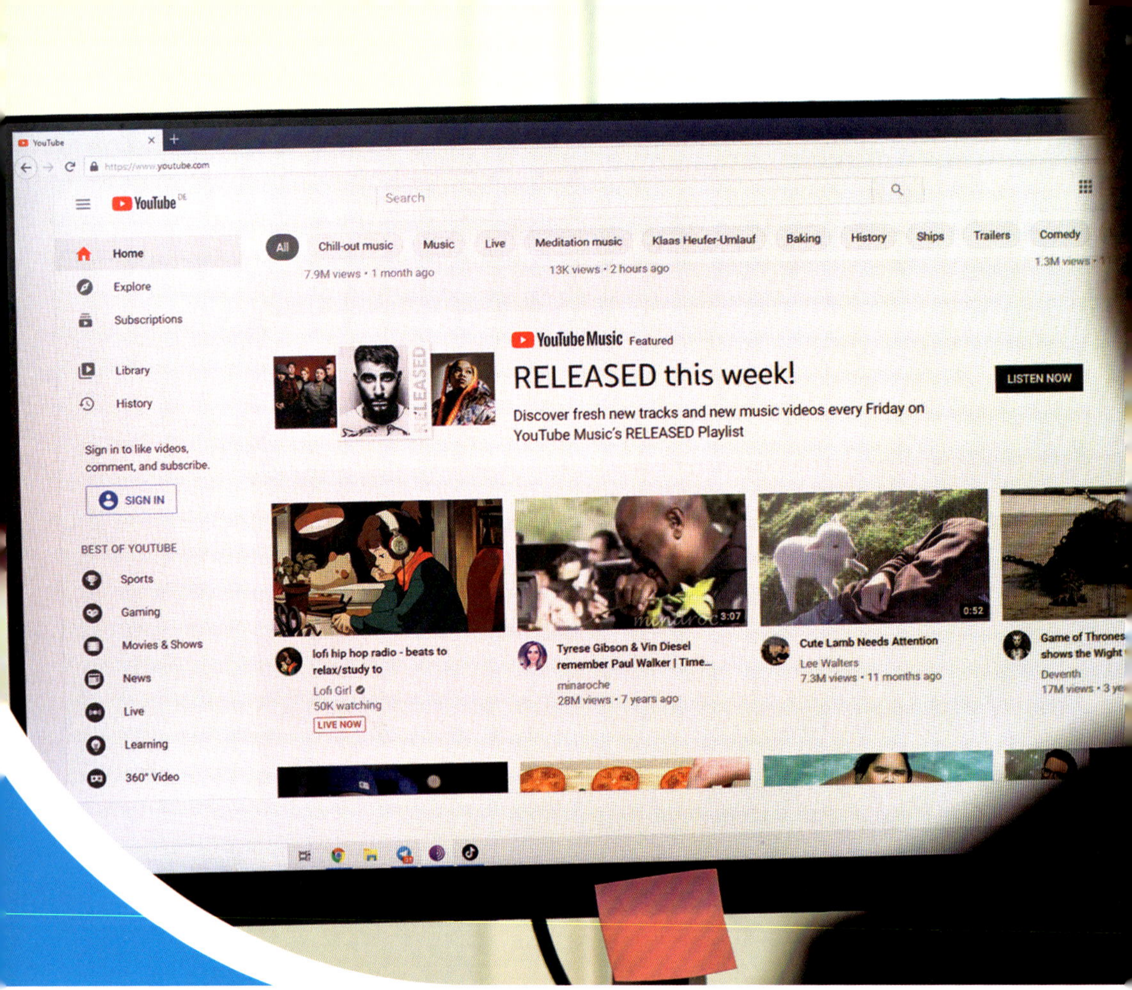

Private companies, such as YouTube, can decide what types of speech are allowed on their sites.

Another limit involves private businesses. Companies can decide what speech is allowed in their spaces. This includes social media companies. In 2019, many YouTube videos had **hate speech**. This went against YouTube's rules. YouTube removed more than 100,000 videos and 17,000 channels. It took down more than 500 million comments. YouTube had the right to do this.

FREEDOM TO OFFEND

It may seem like there are many limits to freedom of speech and the press. But these limits are in place to protect people's rights. The First Amendment protects many kinds of speech. For example, many people think hate speech is illegal. But it is protected by the Constitution. People have the freedom to be rude or mean with their words. William Brennan was on the Supreme Court. He served from 1956 to 1990. He said the government "may not prohibit the expression of an idea simply because society finds the idea itself offensive or disagreeable."[2]

Many court cases involve freedom of speech and the press. Some cases go all the way to the Supreme Court. This is the nation's highest court. It has nine judges. The Supreme Court decides if laws follow the Constitution. It decides what speech is protected.

The Supreme Court hears cases involving freedom of speech and the press. The Supreme Court Building is located in Washington, DC.

Today, the words *speech* and *press* include more than talking and writing. Using the internet and **broadcasting** are forms of expression too. They are also protected by the Constitution.

2

THE HISTORY OF THE FREEDOMS

Freedom of speech and the press was not always guaranteed. Before the Constitution was written, there were thirteen colonies in North America. These colonies were ruled by the king of England. In 1734, freedom of speech was tested in court. Colonist John Peter Zenger published articles criticizing a royal official. It did not matter if Zenger's information was true. He was accused of printing libel and arrested.

During Zenger's trial, the jury surprised the court. It believed Zenger had told the truth. It said he was not guilty. The jury did not follow English law. Instead, it

Freedom of speech was tested during the John Peter Zenger trial. Zenger was found not guilty.

George Mason wrote the Virginia Declaration of Rights. There is a memorial for Mason in Washington, DC.

decided true information was not libel. The Zenger trial did not change English law. But it changed how people thought about freedom of the press.

STARTING WITH THE STATES

About thirty years later, the Revolutionary War (1775–1783) began. The colonists grew tired of being ruled by England. They wanted to govern themselves. Tensions between England and the colonies led to war. The colonists fought for independence from England. During this time, the Continental Congress served as the government.

In 1776, Congress asked the colonies to write their own constitutions. George Mason was part of Virginia's legislature. He thought each state's constitution needed a declaration of rights. Mason wrote the Virginia Declaration of Rights. It included freedom of the press.

In 1776, the colonies declared their independence from England. They became the United States. The new country needed a government. In 1777, Congress created the Articles of Confederation. This was the country's first constitution. But it did not give the national government much power. The states had most of the power. Congress could not tax the states or raise an army. It could not settle disputes between states. The government was weak.

At the Constitutional Convention, the country's founders created a new form of government. George Washington led the convention.

A STRONGER GOVERNMENT

In 1787, **delegates** from each state met in Philadelphia. This meeting was called the Constitutional Convention. The delegates created a new government. They decided on the government's structure. They wrote this in the Constitution. Under the Articles, the government had one branch. Under the Constitution, it would have three branches. These are the legislative, judicial, and executive branches.

The government's powers were divided between the branches. This way, no branch could become too powerful. The legislative branch is Congress. It makes laws. The judicial branch includes the courts. It decides if laws follow the Constitution. The executive branch is led by the president. It makes sure laws are followed.

The Bill of Rights is on display at the National Archives in Washington, DC.

For the new government to be established, the Constitution had to be ratified. This meant nine states had to approve it. But some delegates were not satisfied with the Constitution. George

Mason had suggested a bill of rights. This was not included in the Constitution. Some delegates thought it was not needed. Others thought there were too many rights to include. Thomas Jefferson agreed with Mason. He had written the Declaration of Independence in 1776. This document declared America's freedom from England. Jefferson wrote that "a bill of rights is what the people are entitled to against every government on Earth . . . and what no just government should refuse."[3]

The Constitution was sent to the states for approval. But people thought it needed a bill of rights. They did not trust a strong national government. Finally, the two sides reached an agreement. If the states approved the Constitution, Congress would add a bill of rights. The new government began in 1789. Congress created the Bill of Rights. It became part of the Constitution in 1791.

FROM OPPONENT TO PROMOTER

James Madison was a delegate to the Constitutional Convention. He was a congressman from Virginia. At first, Madison believed the Constitution did not need a bill of rights. But when Congress met, he pushed it to keep its promise to the states. He helped write the Bill of Rights and get it approved.

3

FIGURING OUT THE FREEDOMS

The Bill of Rights guarantees freedom of speech and the press. But those rights have been tested. One early challenge came soon after the Constitution was ratified. In 1798, the United States was facing war with France. There were two political parties. They were called the Democratic-Republicans and the Federalists. The Federalists supported a strong national government. But the Democratic-Republicans criticized the government. The Federalists thought the Democratic-Republicans were disloyal.

John Adams served as president from 1797 to 1801. He was part of the Federalist Party. He signed the Sedition Act of 1798.

There were more Federalists in Congress than Democratic-Republicans. The Federalists passed the Sedition Act. This made it illegal for people to say or print anything bad about the government. Some people criticized the government anyway. They were arrested. James Madison said Congress was using "a power not delegated by the Constitution, but . . . expressly and positively forbidden by one of the amendments thereto."[4] But Congress kept the Sedition Act. It went away when the Federalists lost the next election.

Abolitionists such as Wendell Phillips (pictured) and William Lloyd Garrison were involved in the American Anti-Slavery Society.

CONGRESS TAKES ACTION

During the 1830s, northern and southern states disagreed about slavery. Slavery was a common practice in the United States. Black people were kidnapped from Africa and brought to the United States. In the

Slavery was a common practice in the US South. Many people spoke out against slavery.

South, people forced enslaved people to work on farms.

But in the North, people spoke out against slavery. In 1833, the American Anti-Slavery Society formed. It wanted to end slavery. In 1834, it asked people to send petitions to the US government.

The petitions called for the end of slavery in Washington, DC. Thousands of petitions were sent. In response, Congress passed a gag rule. This banned discussions or debates about ending slavery. John Quincy Adams was a Congress member. He opposed this rule. He said he saw a "conspiracy in and out of Congress to crush the liberties of a free people of the Union."[5] The rule denied the right to petition and free speech. But the gag rule lasted until 1844.

Freedom of speech was also challenged during World War I (1914–1918). This war involved many countries. Some promised to defend each other. The United States entered the war in 1917. It joined the Allied Powers. These were Britain, France, Russia, Japan, and Italy. They fought the Central Powers: Germany, Austria-Hungary, and Turkey. In 1917 and 1918, Congress passed the Espionage and Sedition Acts. These aimed to stop dangerous activities against the government. They made it illegal to criticize the government or military.

TAKING IT TO THE TOP

Many people were accused of breaking the Espionage and Sedition Acts. More than

Justice Oliver Wendell Holmes led the court during the Schenck v. United States case.

2,000 Americans were sent to prison. One was Charles Schenck. He mailed a flyer that opposed the draft. The draft required young men to serve in the military. Schenck's case went to the Supreme Court.

The case was called *Schenck v. United States*. The judges said the Espionage and Sedition Acts followed the Constitution. Oliver Wendell Holmes led the court. He said Schenck's words created "a clear and present danger."[6] His flyer could have hurt the war effort. So he did not have the freedom to write it.

In 1931, the Supreme Court heard the case of *Near v. Minnesota*. This involved a journalist named Jay Near. He was the editor of the *Saturday Press*. He published a series of articles. The articles accused several police officers and city officials of neglecting their duties. One officer took Near to court. He said the articles were **malicious**. But the Supreme Court ruled in favor of the press.

In 1964, another case tested freedom of the press. During this time, many Black

ON THE AIR

Free speech cases may involve broadcasting too. In 1978, the Supreme Court heard the case *Federal Communications Commission (FCC) v. Pacifica Foundation*. The issue was whether the FCC could ban explicit words used on the radio. The court sided with the FCC. It said this speech could be harmful.

***The New York Times* has been reporting on the news since 1851. In 1964, it was found not guilty in a libel case that went to the Supreme Court.**

people were fighting for equal rights. They held protests. The police often used violence against the protesters. Some of the protest leaders placed an ad in the *New York Times*. It made the police look bad. It also contained a false statement about them. The newspaper had not checked the facts. A police officer sued the newspaper for libel. The case was called *New York Times Co. v. Sullivan*.

But the Supreme Court sided with the newspaper. It said the paper did not know the statement was false. So it was not guilty of libel. The Supreme Court judges understood the importance of freedom of speech and the press. Today, judges still make decisions about these rights.

4

UP FOR DEBATE

Freedom of speech and the press is still debated today. This is because the way these rights are understood constantly changes. New technology creates more ways to communicate. This creates questions about which types of speech should be protected.

Free speech is often debated on college campuses. Colleges want to promote free speech. Laura Beth Nielsen is a professor at Northwestern University. She said, "We want our students to feel safe to express their ideas on campus, and we want a

Many colleges promote free speech. They want students to be able to express their ideas.

diversity of opinions to be represented."[7] But students are sometimes afraid to say what they think. They worry about how others will react.

Students' words can also create dangerous situations. Colleges want to keep students safe. Sometimes a student's speech can be threatening. It can disrupt learning. Many believe this speech should be restricted on college campuses.

CANCEL CULTURE

Another issue is cancel culture. This involves **boycotting** or publicly shaming someone.

In 2020, people canceled J.K. Rowling, the author of the Harry Potter books. She had posted harmful comments about transgender people on Twitter.

People may be canceled when they do something questionable. They may be canceled for expressing an unpopular opinion. Canceling began as a way to hold people accountable. Sometimes politicians or celebrities use hateful words. Canceling these people limits their influence. But other people can also be canceled. Today, people can call out anyone online. Because of the internet and social media, anyone can get

CENSORSHIP

Sometimes groups try to prevent people from saying things. They try to keep people from printing words or images. This is called censorship. When the government censors something, freedom of speech may be threatened. But private companies can censor. For example, YouTube can remove videos or comments that contain hate speech.

involved. Sometimes people just cancel others with whom they disagree.

Many people worry about being canceled for their words. Social media makes this more complicated. It can be hard to share ideas. Likes and dislikes on social media posts can affect what people say online. Sometimes people post things that are not meant to harm anyone. But they might get negative comments or insults. Everyone wants to enjoy free speech. But that means people must be willing to hear ideas they do not like.

FREEDOM OF SPEECH VS. SAFETY ONLINE

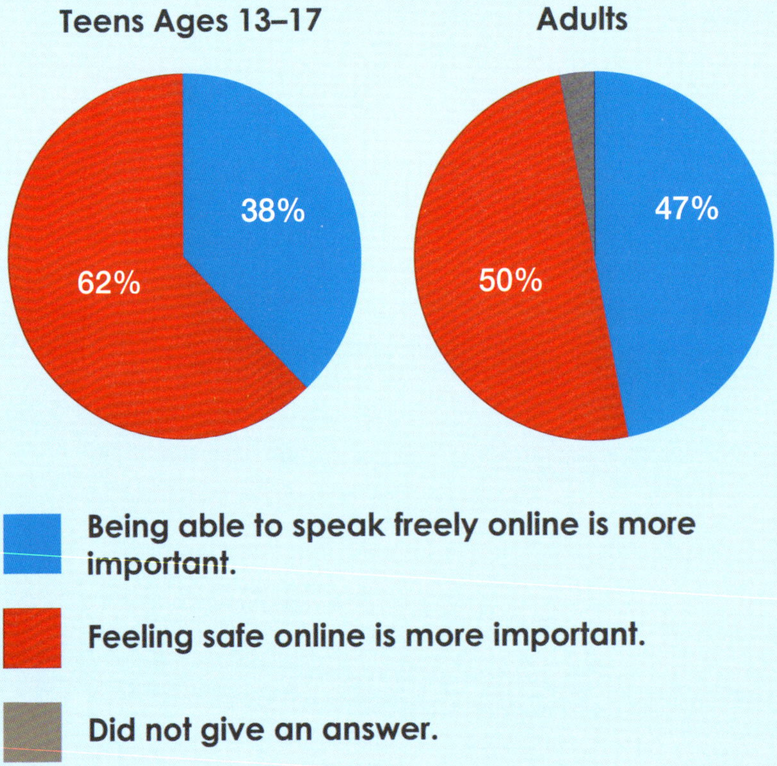

Source: "Majority of U.S. Teens Say People Feeling Welcome and Safe Online Is More Important Than Being Able to Speak Freely," Pew Research Center, *August 29, 2022. www.pewresearch.org.*

A 2022 survey looked at how US teens and adults feel about freedom of speech online. It asked them if feeling safe or speaking freely online was more important.

IN THE COURTROOM

Another issue involves cameras in courtrooms. The press often uses cameras during court cases. This way, they can show people how justice is carried out. But their cameras can disrupt trials.

In 1965, the case *Estes v. Texas* went to the Supreme Court. In Estes's original trial, dozens of camerapeople came into the courtroom. They disrupted the trial. The Supreme Court said the cameras were distracting. The defendant had not received a fair trial. Cameras in court can also invade privacy. People may not want the public

Some people think cameras can disrupt government proceedings. But cameras are allowed in Congress committee hearings and state courts.

watching their trials. Judges decide if cameras will be allowed in a courtroom.

Shield laws are another issue. These say that journalists do not have to reveal their sources. If sources fear their names becoming public, they may stay silent about what they know. This may keep the public from receiving news.

Shield laws are not in the Constitution. In court, journalists have the same duties as others. If needed, journalists may be forced to reveal sources.

Some congresspeople want to help journalists. They want to pass a national shield law. One proposed bill is the Free Flow of Information Act. This would protect journalists who refuse to reveal their sources. As of early 2023, Congress had not yet made the bill into a law.

Richard Lugar was a senator. He served from 1977 to 2013. He said the act would give journalists "certain rights and abilities to seek sources and report appropriate information without fear of intimidation or imprisonment."[8]

It can be hard to balance freedom of speech with other values. These freedoms affect national security. They affect people's safety. Ways of expressing these freedoms will continue to change.

Under shield laws, journalists are not required to reveal their sources.

But understanding the freedoms is the first step in protecting them.

GLOSSARY

boycotting

refusing to buy, use, go to, or support something in order to make a protest

broadcasting

spreading a message over a large area by television, radio, or internet

delegates

people who are chosen to represent others

democratic

relating to or demonstrating the belief that all people should be treated equally

hate speech

speech or writing that expresses prejudice

malicious

having a wish to harm or intending to cause harm

petition

to submit a formal written request to someone in authority

reputation

the beliefs or opinions others have about an individual

SOURCE NOTES

CHAPTER ONE: WHAT IS FREEDOM OF SPEECH?

1. "The Constitution of the United States: A Transcription," *National Archives*, February 3, 2023. www.archives.gov.

2. Quoted in Melissa Beattie-Moss, "Probing Question: Are There Limits to Freedom of Speech?" *PennState*, January 27, 2015. www.psu.edu.

CHAPTER TWO: THE HISTORY OF THE FREEDOMS

3. "To James Madison from Thomas Jefferson, 20 December 1787," *National Archives: Founders Online*, December 20, 1787. https://founders.archives.gov.

CHAPTER THREE: FIGURING OUT THE FREEDOMS

4. Quoted in "Virginia and Kentucky Resolutions (1798)," *Bill of Rights Institute*, December 24, 1798. https://billofrightsinstitute.org.

5. Quoted in "John Quincy Adams and the Gag Rule," *Bill of Rights Institute*, n.d. https://billofrightsinstitute.org.

6. Quoted in "Schenck v. United States (1919)," *National Constitution Center*, n.d. https://constitutioncenter.org.

CHAPTER FOUR: UP FOR DEBATE

7. Quoted in Lisa Stein, "What Does 'Free Speech' Mean on a College Campus?" *Weinberg College of Arts and Sciences*, 2018. https://weinberg.northwestern.edu.

8. Quoted in Michael D. Saperstein Jr., "Federal Shield Law: Protecting Free Speech or Endangering the Nation?" *CommLaw Conspectus*, January 2006. https://scholarship.law.edu.

FOR FURTHER RESEARCH

BOOKS

Ruth Bjorklund, *The Bill of Rights: Why It Matters to You*. New York: Children's Press, 2020.

Janie Havemeyer, *Individual Rights and Liberties*. San Diego, CA: BrightPoint Press, 2024.

Allison Matulli and Clelia Castro-Malaspina, *Your Freedom, Your Power: A Kid's Guide to the First Amendment*. New York: Running Press Kids, 2023.

INTERNET SOURCES

"First Amendment Activities," *United States Courts*, n.d. www.uscourts.gov.

"The Bill of Rights: What Does It Say?" *National Archives*, February 15, 2022. www.archives.gov.

"What Is the First Amendment?" *First Amendment Museum*, n.d. https://firstamendmentmuseum.org.

WEBSITES

Ben's Guide to the US Government
https://bensguide.gpo.gov

Ben's Guide to the US Government features information, games, and learning activities about the federal government.

First Amendment Museum
https://firstamendmentmuseum.org

The First Amendment Museum website provides information and activities about the First Amendment.

United States Courts
www.uscourts.gov

The United States Courts website features information and learning resources about the US courts.

INDEX

IMAGE CREDITS

Cover: © monkeybusinessimages/iStockphoto
5: © Andreas Stroh/Shutterstock Images
7: © Big Tuna Online/Shutterstock Images
8: © Koshiro K/Shutterstock Images
10: © Lya_Cattel/iStockphoto
13: © spxChrome/iStockphoto
15: © Steve Sanchez Photos/Shutterstock Images
16: © Gim42/iStockphoto
20: © Postmodern Studio/Shutterstock Images
23: © Rob Crandall/Shutterstock Images
25: © Library of Congress
26: © Rob Crandall/Shutterstock Images
29: © Everett Collection/Shutterstock Images
31: © Joe Sohm/Visions of America, LLC/Alamy
35: © Everett Collection/Shutterstock Images
37: © Library of Congress
38: © ilbusca/iStockphoto
41: © Library of Congress
44: © Hadrian/Shutterstock Images
47: © Leigh Trail/Shutterstock Images
49: © Fred Duval/Shutterstock Images
52: © Red Line Editorial
54: © Mark Reinstein/Shutterstock Images
57: © LightField Studios/Shutterstock Images

ABOUT THE AUTHOR

Samantha S. Bell lives in the foothills of the Blue Ridge Mountains with her family and too many cats. She is the author of more than 150 nonfiction books for kids. She loves learning about American history. It was her favorite subject all through school.